LOW

AN HONEST ADVENT DEVOTIONAL

JOHN PAVLOVITZ

D1115693

chalice press

Saint Louis, Missouri

An imprint of Christian Board of Publication

Cover design: Jennifer Pavlovitz

ChalicePress.com

Print: 9780827221932
EPUB: 9780827221949   EPDF: 9780827221956

Printed in the United States of America

Contents

Introduction

We naturally read the Bible retrospectively. We encounter our faith tradition in the rearview mirror of history, and as a result we approach it knowing how the story ends. This often leads us to sanitize the gospels—to obscure the gritty, messy reality of those moments as they were experienced in real time. We tend to over-spiritualize the events being described, and we view the God-narrative as if from 30 thousand feet, safe in the abstract places of detached theology. Scripture is a movie we are passively watching rather than a story we are participating in, and so we often miss the gravity of moments, failing to experience them on a visceral level.

But there is a beauty in trying to see these accounts from the ground level, to imagine how they looked and felt from the low places of people's ordinary lives. When we do this, we remember what is really going on here. We remember that this is the story of an olive-skinned baby, born amid the smell of damp straw and animal dung because no human-worthy welcome could be found; of a child of young Palestinian Jewish parents, desperately fleeing politically ordered genocide. It is the story of a poor, itinerant, street preaching rabbi spending his days dining with the lepers and prostitutes, enlisting the doubters and the backsliders, and comforting the bleeding and the grieving. It is divinity coming low to inhabit humanity.

When we place our feet firmly in the dirt and dust of the everyday within the gospel stories, we see Jesus getting low to meet us there. The spiritual journey is spent largely in the low and shadow places. We are there in that beautiful lowness when we live humbly. We are there when we seek forgiveness. We are there in our grief and suffering. We are there when we kneel in reverent awe. We are there when we spend ourselves on behalf of someone else. When we place ourselves in these postures, our perspective changes, our attitude toward people shifts, and we become agents of love in a way that actually resembles Jesus. We perpetuate his character through our very lives.

When Jesus offers the prayer, "Thy kingdom come, thy will be done, on earth as it is in heaven," he reminds us that as we walk the road of Advent the invitation is not to escape this place to an elevated heavenly sanctuary somewhere; it is to bring heaven down. Immanuel means "God with us." In other words, it is Jesus getting low. This is really good news for us here on the ground.

Let's head to the low places together.

A Messy Nativity

While they were there, the time came for the baby to be born, and she gave birth to her firstborn, a son.

—LUKE 2:6–7

I still remember witnessing my wife giving birth to our first child, Noah. The wait of the previous nine months had seemed agonizingly slow, but during those final moments in the hospital, everything accelerated to a velocity approaching light speed. After warnings that his arrival was imminent, I'd been quickly ushered into a closet-sized space adjacent to the delivery room and instructed to don a white outfit that seemed part HAZMAT suit, part late-Elvis stage jumpsuit sans the bedazzling. Just as I was finishing fastening myself in, I was led to my wife's side, where I essentially became a passionate, well-meaning—though incidental— spectator. Up until that point, I thought I'd prepared myself. I'd attended all the classes along with her, had countless lengthy conversations about what to expect, and read all the requisite books to feel properly equipped for what I was about witness. I had no idea.

The sounds and scents and sights were the kind of disorienting sensory overload that transcends words. I stayed upright—but barely.

We tend to sanitize the birth story of Jesus, fashioning it into a pristine, shimmering nativity scene adorned with gold accents and residing comfortably on a hallway table or atop a fireplace mantle. It all becomes so benign and serene that we forget the visceral reality of the moment, that it was as loud and chaotic and messy as childbirth is. Jesus was pushed through Mary's birth canal and into a strange world. To miss this fact is to cheapen the event by trying to soften it into something neat and orderly, when in truth (as with all births) there was surely mess and chaos in the moment.

We do this with our spiritual journeys too, wanting them to be comfortable and clean, desiring something attractive that we can easily accessorize our lives with— but that isn't reality, is it? Life comes with the collateral damage of living, with failed plans and relational collapse, with internal struggle and existential crises, and we carry these things with us into this season. The good news is we don't need to discard our messiness to step into this season, and we couldn't even if we wanted to. Bring every bit of your flawed self and all your chaotic circumstances to this day. Welcome the mess.

Faith in the Intersection

> *As Jesus was walking beside the Sea of Galilee,*
> *he saw two brothers, Simon called Peter and his*
> *brother Andrew. They were casting a net into*
> *the lake, for they were fishermen. "Come, follow*
> *me," Jesus said, "and I will send you out to*
> *fish for people." At once they left their nets and*
> *followed him.*
>
> —MATTHEW 4:18–20

I lived on the planet for 26 years before I met my wife. My road twisted and pinballed for a quarter of a century with me not knowing she even existed—until one day, there we were sharing the same space and time in a college classroom in Philadelphia. Our long and very separate journeys suddenly overlapped, and we didn't know it at first, but everything in our lives would be different. All of our relationships can be understood as intersections: the places our road meets that of another person and both stories are rewritten, sometimes wonderfully and sometimes less so. Each of us is a product of these many crossings.

I always liked the idea of reading the gospel stories and looking for the intersections—the times Jesus' life crossed the path of another person—and how each person was irrevocably changed by the occasion. A man driven to madness and isolation finds rest in his own head. A shunned leper receives an unprecedented embrace. A woman caught in adultery is surprised by extraordinary mercy. A despised tax collector is invited into revolutionary ministry. A man four days dead is raised to life again. A young, terrified woman is asked to bear a planet-rocking baby. Over and over, when someone meets Jesus, transformation and restoration are waiting; there is something wondrous to be witnessed. The very birth narrative of Jesus is the image of the most profound of intersections: God and earth meeting, and the latter being completely altered.

Today, dwell on the people who've crossed your circuitous path and changed your story. Remember some of those initial meetings and the ground you've covered since. Sit with gratitude for them and for the difference they've made on your journey. And reflect on the way you've been changed by an encounter with God—or what seemed like God to you in that moment. Think about the love and the faith you've found in the intersections.

This Is Not a Test

He told them still another parable: "The kingdom of heaven is like yeast that a woman took and mixed into about sixty pounds of flour until it worked all through the dough." Jesus spoke all these things to the crowd in parables; he did not say anything to them without using a parable. So was fulfilled what was spoken through the prophet:

"I will open my mouth in parables,
    I will utter things hidden since the creation of the world."

—Matthew 13:33–35

At one point in my spiritual journey, I reached a place where every infinitesimal decision seemed like a specific moral test, a perpetual pass-fail pop quiz from God that I needed to get precisely right—or else. (The "or else" usually involved heat, humidity, and endless teeth gnashing.) I continually agonized over trying to hear what God was telling me in the most benign of moments (since so many other Christians I knew seemed so adept at it, from what they told me). In this heavily pressurized headspace, God's will became a singular, microscopic needle in a planet-sized haystack that I was required to find over and over again, or risk punishment. It was exhausting and frustrating, and it tended to make me miserable. As I started to read the gospels more closely, I discovered something new there: *mystery*. Instead of hard-and-fast rules, I found curious word pictures about yeast inside dough, seeds scattered into soil, branches connected to vines, and treasures buried underground. I found nebulous calls to meekness and heart purity and peacemaking. As I embraced that wonder, I felt freer in the expansive space of daily life.

Jesus didn't need to *live* here. He could have shown up, tossed out another stone slab or a rolled parchment filled with black-and-white religious do's and don'ts, and then disappeared into the ether—leaving a neat and tidy, easily navigable religion to delineate our every decision. Instead, he chose to live life alongside flawed human beings, in messy and meandering trips into wheatfields and lepers' homes and leaky boats.

There is a great deal of gray (or color) in this low-to-the-ground spiritual journey. The birth (and the life) of Jesus remind us that our daily existence is not a precise theological test, and the goal is not to avoid failing. It is an ever-unfolding trip through a day we've never been to, where we notice beauty, move with compassion, have grace revealed, and within a wide and expansive space—we get to choose.

Too Good to Be True?

But the angel said to them, "Do not be afraid. I bring you good news that will cause great joy for all the people."

—Luke 2:10

I tend to be skeptical of late-night infomercials. I know they're trying to sell me something, and it makes the lofty claims their enthusiastic (and somehow always Australian) spokespeople deliver pretty tough to swallow. They usually promise far more in matters of internal transformation and emotional well-being than a simple toaster oven or garden hose should be able to deliver—and most of the time I see right through them, because I know that I'll be disappointed if I fall for it. Of course, there are those occasions when the sales pitch is perfectly presented and hits me at just the right time (usually when I'm hungry or bored or open to suggestion) and I make a purchase. Four to six weeks later when the product arrives, I'm usually disappointed.

Good news. Great Joy. All people. Those are the unbelievable claims of the angels to the shepherds about what one coming child will bring with him. It sounds like a pretty lofty list of features for one nondescript baby born in a feeding trough to make good on—and the shepherds would have been justified in making a hard pass. Perhaps the fact that they too witnessed this spectacular sales pitch at night explains their immediate enthusiasm. Whatever the reason, the shepherds were all in and soon became passionate pitchmen themselves.

Two thousand years after this first angelic info-mercial, we who seek to perpetuate Jesus here have to wrestle with the reality that the people of Jesus have not always been good news or great joy to all people. We have to decide if those failures are overpromises or just user error. Is our faith tradition able to be all we hope it will be? Can we deliver on the promises made by the angels? Can we supply the world with something that—surprisingly—isn't too good to be true?

So many people in vulnerable communities are rightly skeptical that such beauty exists in this story because of the ugliness Christians have shown them, and because of the injustices and cruelties they experience. Today, look for direct, tangible, and close ways to bring news that is good, and joy that is great, to all people in your path.

Fleeing to Egypt

When they had gone, an angel of the Lord appeared to Joseph in a dream. "Get up," he said, "take the child and his mother and escape to Egypt. Stay there until I tell you, for Herod is going to search for the child to kill him." So he got up, took the child and his mother during the night and left for Egypt, where he stayed until the death of Herod. And so was fulfilled what the Lord had said through the prophet: "Out of Egypt I called my son."

—MATTHEW 2:13–15

I walked around today and I looked at people: those passing me in the grocery store, driving beside me on the highway, filling my newsfeed, walking by the house. I tried to really *see* them, to look beneath the surface veneer they wore, to imagine the invisible burdens they might be carrying below the surface: sick children, relational collapse, financial tension, crippling depression, profound grief, crisis of faith, loss of purpose—or maybe just their own customized multitude of nagging insecurities and fears they've been carrying around since grade school and have never been able to shake. As I looked at all these people, I wondered what kind of specific and personal hell they might be enduring, and what it might be doing to them inside.

We are seeing an epidemic of cruelty in these days, a lack of empathy that leaves people feeling more alone than ever before. So many of the grieving, struggling, fearful human beings filling up the landscape we find ourselves in today are hanging by the very thinnest of threads. They are heroically pushing back despair, enduring real and imagined terrors, warring with their external circumstances *and* their internal demons. They are doing the very best they can, sometimes with little help or hope, and they need those of us who live alongside them to make that *best-doing* a little easier. This is when we bend low to meet them where their pain lives. It is where Jesus' feet always led him.

Every person around you has their Herod—that terrifying and persistent thing that assails them, the relentless fear-bringer that will not let them rest. With a listening ear or an act of simple kindness, step into their urgency and their unrest today. Bring the hope that offers them escape and helps them see a day beyond this one—and find a way to get them to Egypt.

Eyes on the Road

"Ask and it will be given to you; seek and you will find; knock and the door will be opened to you."
—MATTHEW 7:7

Growing up in Syracuse, New York, I heard the phrase "lake effect snow" at a very early age. The condition develops when air moves across large expanses of water (the Great Lakes); picks up moisture from lower, warmer layers of air; and moves it into the colder air above, freezing it and swiftly depositing it on land in large quantities of frozen precipitation. But I never knew this when I was younger, and I really didn't care for the meteorological explanation. I just knew that it often snowed—a lot. I have countless memories of driving in sudden and complete whiteouts on rapidly disappearing roads that only a few moments earlier had been clear and unobstructed. It took every bit of attention to keep from sliding off the pavement and into the encroaching drifts beside us. You'd often arrive at your destination with your fingers cramped from white-knuckling the wheel the whole way, and perhaps a bit out of breath—but most of the time you made it safely. Turns out that when you're that invested in a task, you tend to do pretty well.

Many years ago as a young youth leader, I was talking with my pastor about the future (one I was overly worried about), and he said, "John, do you know why a bluebird finds worms? Because that's what it looks for." He told me that much of what we discover in this life is about the questions we ask, the things we give attention to, and the way we invest our time. He reassured me that the more aware I was of the orientation of my life at any given moment, and the more intentional I was along the way, the more I could rest in knowing I'd eventually end up where I need to be. It's a truth I've held onto ever since: the spiritual journey isn't always one of seeing in real time, but about paying attention in the present, and the eventual arrival. This helps me when the road gets obscured and the way forward is difficult to spot.

Today you may be unsure of the road ahead, feeling fruitless in your efforts, or hopeless in the moment. Keep going. Rest in the knowledge that even in the squalls and whiteouts and places where the path seems unclear, you'll end up where you need to be.

Carry and Deliver

In the sixth month of Elizabeth's pregnancy,
God sent the angel Gabriel to Nazareth, a town
in Galilee, to a virgin pledged to be married to a
man named Joseph, a descendant of David. The
virgin's name was Mary. The angel went to her
and said, "Greetings, you who are highly favored!
The Lord is with you." Mary was greatly troubled
at his words and wondered what kind of greeting
this might be. But the angel said to her, "Do not
be afraid, Mary; you have found favor with God.
You will conceive and give birth to a son, and you
are to call him Jesus. He will be great and will be
called the Son of the Most High. The Lord God
will give him the throne of his father David, and
he will reign over Jacob's descendants forever; his
kingdom will never end."

—LUKE 1:26–33

Growing up Catholic, I understood Mary the mother of Jesus very differently than I do today. When I was younger, she held this place of rarefied adoration that, while reverential, almost obscured the earthy reality of her part in the story: the uncertainty and scandal in which she'd found herself. Largely lost on me was the fact that she was a young girl, already engaged, and suddenly with child of unfathomable origin—living surrounded by ordinary people who didn't read her story with the detached hindsight we have. The fear and the pressure of her circumstances would have been disorienting. She was invited into something beautifully terrifying, and she simply said, "Yes."

As I've gotten older, I've focused on Mary's *yes* in that moment, the way she accepted the invitation she'd been given, knowing it would also mean welcoming opposition. Today I see her as an ancestor in this journey, the first responder for those of us who seek to emulate Jesus in the world. Mary was asked to literally *carry and deliver* the love of God to a planet in dire need of such a thing. She willingly accepted the collateral damage of bearing goodness in a time and place in which doing so would prove difficult.

You and I get to play a similar role in this moment in the story of the planet, a place burdened with sadness and disconnect. We are similarly pregnant with a capacity to bring peace and kindness and healing. Today, think about the character traits of Jesus that resonate most deeply with you (especially those that seem lacking in the world), and realize that these are what you are invited to birth into the world: compassion, forgiveness, courage, honesty. Let goodness form within you today, and find a way to release it into the world.

Sorry and Sorrow

[Jesus] took Peter, James and John along with him, and he began to be deeply distressed and troubled. "My soul is overwhelmed with sorrow to the point of death," he said to them. "Stay here and keep watch." Going a little farther, he fell to the ground and prayed that if possible the hour might pass from him.

—MARK 14:33–35

As I mentioned previously, we don't often think of the stories of Jesus' adult life and ministry as we prepare to celebrate his arrival—and we certainly don't consider moments like this one: Jesus filled with anguish and pressed to what seems like an emotional breaking point—Jesus at his lowest. That scene doesn't lend itself to greeting cards, ornaments, or Christmas hymns, but it probably should. I think we need to remind ourselves not only of Jesus' humanity but also of the very real depths he would go to after arriving. He would end up desperately fearful in prayer. He would find himself deeply grieving the loss of his friend Lazarus. He would be enraged enough to flip the tables of the temple vendors. He would be exasperated with his hardheaded students.

This morning I started typing the word "sorrow," and before I could finish, my computer changed it to "sorry." I know computers don't have religious biases, but as a lifelong Christian, I think that sounds about right. We often feel like we need to apologize for (or at the very least conceal) our lowest points, our deepest anguish, our most human moments—as if such abrasive things are inappropriate or unwelcome, as if they somehow need to wait outside while we pretend that all is merry and bright within and around us.

I love seeing Jesus at his lowest, and to hold such moments in my heart this season, because it reminds me to make room for my sadness and my grief. Christmas is as much the valley as the mountaintop. It is the wedding celebration and it is the funeral procession. It is a joyous, expectant birth, but it's also feeling troubled to the point of death. You get to have all of it. Today, sit with the full breadth of your story—and don't be sorry for your sorrow.

Church Clothes

Therefore, as God's chosen people, holy and dearly loved, clothe yourselves with compassion, kindness, humility, gentleness and patience. Bear with each other and forgive one another if any of you has a grievance against someone. Forgive as the Lord forgave you. And over all these virtues put on love, which binds them all together in perfect unity.

—Colossians 3:12–14

As a young boy, I hated getting dressed up for church. I can distinctly remember lying on my bed on a Sunday morning listening to music or reading comic books, and getting the dreaded call from outside my bedroom door or from downstairs: "Get changed for church!" It was like being called to the principal's office (not that I had any firsthand experience of such things). There was something frustrating about taking off whatever I'd been wearing (which I was quite at home in), and putting on stiff, uncomfortable clothes that I never wore except for that hour on Sunday. "Who are we trying to impress?" I thought to myself. Even then I couldn't imagine God having a dress code, so it always seemed like the sudden change was really about being acceptable to the people around us at church. I quickly recognized the hypocrisy of what a pastor friend once called "The Amazing Grace Face"—people putting on a showy display of perfection and holding the façade together just long enough to make it to the car. The moment I got home, I'd rocket up the stairs and be out of my church clothes in seconds—and back to being myself.

Many of us have had a similar experience with religious systems or spiritual community: the awareness that whoever we normally were wasn't quite suitable, that we'd have to make some surface alterations if we wanted to be fully welcomed. The apostle Paul writes to a group of Jesus followers in Colossae, reminding them of the only necessary attire: compassion, kindness, humility, gentleness, patience, love. These things don't come easily, but they also don't require us to change depending on our environment. We don't have to prove our worth or earn our inclusion. When we're cultivating these values internally, people will naturally experience them as they encounter us. Today, don't worry about the surface things and don't feel pressured to impress anyone. Instead, put on Love—and simply come as you are.

The Curb

Jesus said: "A man was going down from Jerusalem to Jericho, when he was attacked by robbers. They stripped him of his clothes, beat him and went away, leaving him half dead. A priest happened to be going down the same road, and when he saw the man, he passed by on the other side. So too, a Levite, when he came to the place and saw him, passed by on the other side.But a Samaritan, as he traveled, came where the man was; and when he saw him, he took pity on him."
—LUKE 10:30–33

For years I lived in the heart of Philadelphia (what the locals refer to as "Center City"). When I first arrived there as a bright-eyed college freshman, I looked at people I passed on the street—as this seemed a perfectly reasonable tactic. I learned pretty quickly that this was unusual and often ill-advised. People who commuted on foot every day didn't usually make eye contact. They were either too busy to be bothered or too preoccupied with their own lives—and besides, looking into people's eyes meant there was a good chance you'd be asked for help.

Sometimes the plea was direct, but more often there was an elaborate story: a (supposed) broken down car on some neighboring street, or a sudden family emergency that required immediate attention. At first I stopped for every person who implored me—listening intently, offering whatever I had in my pocket, and feeling genuinely concerned. But gradually I began to move people along quickly, rushing them to the point of *the ask* without caring to hear their story, much less sifting it for truth. I grew less and less patient with these distractions in my day, almost resenting them, until finally I learned to do what all the other city walkers did: I looked away. I developed that tunnel vision gaze that stares just off in the distance, pretending it can't see anything closer and lower than a spot upon the horizon. I intentionally stopped seeing people.

Jesus tells the story that's familiar to many of us about a man beaten and robbed and left at the side of the road. We learn that at least two religious people pass by him. (They likely had that same look in their eyes that I learned in Philadelphia.) The hero of this story is the Samaritan who shows mercy. He sees his neighbor (the one who was low) in the gutter and responds. We can welcome this season by turning our gaze downward, by stopping to see people, by allowing ourselves to be inconvenienced by the pain in our path without looking away. See those who are low around you and share the mercy that others may never care enough to show.

Living Parables

He called a little child to him, and placed the child among them. And he said: "Truly I tell you, unless you change and become like little children, you will never enter the kingdom of heaven. Therefore, whoever takes the lowly position of this child is the greatest in the kingdom of heaven."

—Matthew 18:2–4

The adage is true that when you have children, you see the world again through their eyes. Almost by osmosis you absorb some of their wonder, their optimism, their simple, undistracted joy in the present—things that tend to be elusive as you become a proper adult. When you're with them, you also (at least temporarily) discard the idea of the ordinary, because such a concept doesn't exist to a child. Every moment is a revelation, every experience some new breath-stealing discovery. My daughter regularly finds herself agog and wide-eyed at things I long ago stopped giving a second look to: the veins of a leaf, frost on the morning grass, the shape of a cloud. I can't remember the last time I gave a cloud a second glance, and that bothers me.

The older we get, the more wonder-deprived we tend to become. I think the Jesus who comes low understood this, which is why his parables inserted miracles into the mundane. The kingdom of God was treasure hidden in a field; it was a seed falling into good soil; it was yeast working quietly through the dough; it was sparrows and wildflowers and pearls. It would have been impossible for his listeners to experience their ordinary days the same way after hearing him. I imagine that's a bit of what he meant when he talked about embracing the greater life by becoming a child.

You may not have the luxury of serving as sidekick to a toddler today, but maybe you could spend some time today getting low: renew your outlook or alter your vantage point or change your posture so you can see again the ordinary things you may be overlooking. God may meet you there.

The Song You're Singing

But I will sing of your strength,
in the morning I will sing of your love;
for you are my fortress,
my refuge in times of trouble.

You are my strength, I sing praise to you;
you, God, are my fortress,
my God on whom I can rely.

—PSALM 59:16–17

On Thanksgiving Day, the turkey is barely digested when the Christmas music arrives. Some people welcome the seasonal soundtrack warmly, while others begin counting the days until the calendar is flipped and they can be free from the yearly sonic assault. I usually identify with the former, though my playlists vary greatly. Some days I gravitate toward bittersweet ballads, other times I revel in the exuberant children's songs. I sometimes feel perfectly at home in the carols of my faith tradition; other times I run from them.

The book of Psalms has always been a place of comfort for me because of the expansive space the psalms provide. Some are congregational songs written about God to people in a community; others are private journals about the faith journey; still others are solitary prayers composed and delivered directly to God. At times the writer gives praise or offers expressions of gratitude. Other times the psalmist questions whether God is listening or even there at all. The author is all over the map: faithful, doubting, grateful, angry, joyful, depressed. This makes sense to me. I understand the vacillation and inconsistency and those erratic mood swings.

The sprawling nature of the Psalm songbook frees us from the lie that there is a singular expression of faith or a proper way to be on this spiritual journey. We don't have to be happy or have it all figured out or be confident. In fact we can be pretty angry, and if God is God, then God can handle it. We are invited into a complex, paradoxical, contradictory spirituality—into the messiness and the tension between belief and doubt, between joy and despair, between celebration and grief. How do you come to this season? What song are you singing?

Surprise Party

"No one sews a patch of unshrunk cloth on an old garment, for the patch will pull away from the garment, making the tear worse. Neither do people pour new wine into old wineskins. If they do, the skins will burst; the wine will run out and the wineskins will be ruined. No, they pour new wine into new wineskins, and both are preserved."
—Matthew 9:16–17

I'm a control freak. That is to say I don't do surprises well. Like someone you know (perhaps even yourself), I do what I can to limit the unexpected in my life because I like the illusion of control, and because ultimately I believe my plans are the best ones—even if life tends to frequently argue otherwise. I woke up today (as I do on most days) with a certain set of expectations about what might unfold, feeling passionately committed to seeing that agenda come to fruition. I imagine you did too.

The birth of Jesus is one of the greatest surprises ever on the planet. Those awaiting the arrival of a Messiah were expecting a high and mighty warrior or a towering political figure: someone who would come, sword in hand, to right every wrong, to give the powerful their comeuppance, and to rescue the downtrodden. Enter instead a child—conceived in mystery, born in anonymity, and surrounded by people of little renown. That was unexpected. But these would not be the only surprises associated with Jesus' presence. He would grow to teach of the wisdom of childlikeness, the elevated status of humility, the counterintuitive love of one's enemies.

Who Jesus would become, and the kind of life he would call his followers to lead, was the ultimate script-flip—and many people couldn't adjust. The religious leaders then (as now), were so preoccupied with morally policing the world that they ended up missing Love when it showed up in a different package than the one they'd planned on receiving. This would become a pattern in the stories told about Jesus: a ministry of surprise, the last being first, the tax collectors and prostitutes becoming the early adopters, the Samaritans and soldiers and "sinners" serving as the examples. The older I've gotten, the more willing I've become to receive blessing and wisdom and beauty in unexpected places and people, to experience God showing up when it seemed most unlikely. Today, allow yourself to let go of your expectations—of this season, of people, of God. Welcome a love that surprises.

Do What You Can

While he was in Bethany, reclining at the table in the home of Simon the Leper, a woman came with an alabaster jar of very expensive perfume, made of pure nard. She broke the jar and poured the perfume on his head. Some of those present were saying indignantly to one another, "Why this waste of perfume? It could have been sold for more than a year's wages and the money given to the poor." And they rebuked her harshly. "Leave her alone," said Jesus. "Why are you bothering her? She has done a beautiful thing to me. The poor you will always have with you, and you can help them any time you want. But you will not always have me. She did what she could. She poured perfume on my body beforehand to prepare for my burial. Truly I tell you, wherever the gospel is preached throughout the world, what she has done will also be told, in memory of her."
—MARK 14:3–9

No matter how content or grateful or well-adjusted we are, most of us suffer from some level of comparison sickness. Though we'd say otherwise if anyone asked us, we spend an inordinate amount of time placing our lives up against other people's and wondering why we don't measure up. We look at our houses and waistlines and hairlines and marriages and careers and children, never as they are but always in relation to everyone around us. And since we know well the devils of our own details, it's tempting to idealize other people's unknowns until we feel perpetually less-than, never quite measuring up, always in deficit. The arrival of Christmas seems to bring with it an even greater pressure to keep such an unreasonable pace.

This story from Mark's gospel tells us the pressure is imagined. Jesus encounters a woman who is low in stature and in state, and he does not look down on her, though the crowd does. In the presence of those who would condemn her as wasteful, he comes to her defense with the simple declaration: *She did what she could.* It reminds us of the sufficiency of our labors; much like the exasperated woman barging in and breaking a bottle of perfume, we too are doing a beautiful thing in the space of our daily lives. Our desperate and messy efforts are not in vain, even when they feel as such.

Something may seem in disarray right now: your marriage, your career, your relationship with your middle school child, your very belief. Today, rest surrounded by the broken shards of your best efforts, and trust that it is a beautiful thing.

Turbulence Is Coming

*Then Jesus' disciples said; "Now you are speaking
clearly and without figures of speech. Now we
can see that you know all things and that you do
not even need to have anyone ask you questions.
This makes us believe that you came from God."
"Do you now believe?" Jesus replied. "A time is
coming and in fact has come when you will be
scattered, each to your own home. You will leave
me all alone. Yet I am not alone, for my Father
is with me. I have told you these things, so that
in me you may have peace. In this world you will
have trouble. But take heart! I have overcome the
world."*

—JOHN 16:29–33

Recently I was on a flight to Albuquerque, New
Mexico, and I was enjoying the flight (as much as one
can enjoy a flight when they're certain they will die on
an airplane), when I was interrupted by the voice of
the captain. I know it was the captain, because he said,
"Uh, folks, Captain speaking here. I'm going to ask the
flight attendants to suspend our beverage service and
ask you to return to your seats and fasten your seatbelts,

because we're about to hit a little chop… It may get a little choppy."

"Choppy." I've heard that word before. It's never good news. Choppy is captain-speak for "We're about to be shaken like a snow globe in the hands of an angry toddler!" Choppy means I'm about to face my mortality once again while wedged between two strangers. Choppy means I am about to make a lot of promises to God about what I'll do if we land safely—none of which I intend to keep. The captain was telling us matter-of-factly: "Hold on. Prepare yourselves. Turbulence is coming."

This should be familiar territory for us. We are, at all times, experiencing the shaking of being human. I bet you can name exactly what and who the turbulence is for you right now. As Jesus readies his students for his physical absence, he says to them (and to us), "In this world you will have trouble." In other words, "Hold on. Prepare yourselves. Turbulence is coming." But Jesus reminds us that he has overcome, and that we should not be shaken into hopelessness. He, much like the pilot of my plane, is not overwhelmed because he has the threat right-sized. We can do the same.

The question isn't whether we will be placed in storms, but rather, how much of the turbulence we will allow to be placed within us. When we find ourselves in these storms or circumstances or troubling thoughts, we can rest in the knowledge that the things that cause our shaking, in the eyes of a God who sees and loves and accompanies us—are nothing more than a little *chop*.

The Lowest Places

"Forget the former things;
  do not dwell on the past.
See, I am doing a new thing!
  Now it springs up; do you not perceive it?
I am making a way in the wilderness
  and streams in the wasteland."
—Isaiah 43:18–19

They say you can't teach an old dog new tricks. I'm not sure what the cutoff age for that adage is, but now nearing 50, I sometimes feel I'm getting terrifyingly close. I'm a whole lot less adventurous than I used to be. In matters of technology or music or activities or diet, I tend to stick with what I know, feeling more and more resistant to new things. The familiar allows me control, and this control provides comfort—and like most old dogs, I like comfort. When I do venture into uncharted territory, I feel the easy frustration that comes with being stretched beyond my preferences.

You have heard it said, but I tell you...

Jesus has a way of stretching us. Over and over again in the gospels, the message he has for those who would emulate him in the world, is, in essence, "I want to show you something new. Whatever standard you once used for how to live and treat people and find meaning, I'm asking you for more—(or rather, for *less*)." Regarding anger or motive or religion or revenge or comfort, he continually invites us to the low places: to a greater humility, to a deeper forgiveness, to a shrinking ego, to a bigger generosity. We almost always resist such things because initially they feel like loss, like we're giving up too much, like we're letting someone else get away with something. But we always find a better version of ourselves in the low places and that is why we need to keep going there.

Today, as you walk deeper into this season, reflect on what part of your mind, heart, or life you are avoiding stretching, or in what situation you are resistant to setting aside your ego. Embrace a new thing.

Twisted Bowels

Jesus went through all the towns and villages, teaching in their synagogues, proclaiming the good news of the kingdom and healing every disease and sickness. When he saw the crowds, he had compassion on them, because they were harassed and helpless, like sheep without a shepherd.

—MATTHEW 9:35–36

The word *compassion* used in the scripture above has its roots in the Greek word for "bowels," the idea that we could be so moved by the suffering of others as to be internally altered to the point of sickness—to be twisted up inside. In other words, when we see others experiencing the low points of this life (grief, pain, injustice, loss), we too allow ourselves to become low and sit with them. This vicarious distress is at the heart of the birth narrative of Jesus—God seeing suffering and coming low to meet people in their sorrow—and it would be what marked Jesus' life and ministry. Jesus always sought proximity to people who were hurting or alone or in need, and he was always there grieving alongside them, tending to their wounds, making them feel seen. In this way, his was a *low life*, and his willingness to carry and embrace the heartache of others speaks to a glaring gap in the world, one that can only be filled with compassion.

The sheer scale of suffering today can tend to overwhelm us, which is why compassion is in such great demand and why we need to practice empathy relentlessly. One of the greatest ways we can prepare is to keep our hearts soft even though so many others' have become hardened, and to not lose the desire nor the ability to be powerfully moved by the pain in our path. It is a fitting way to walk into this season of Advent, asking, "Where is the burden? What bothers me? What twists my bowels to the point of sickness?" As we answer these questions and are willing to move in response, we perpetuate Jesus here. Today, see the suffering around you and let yourself be twisted.

Closing Doors

[Mary] wrapped him in cloths and placed him in a manger, because there was no guest room available for them.

—LUKE 2:7

I travel quite a bit, and often, despite my best efforts, I find myself somewhere overloaded with suitcases, falling behind and breathlessly running toward quickly closing elevator doors, hoping kindness from the other side will reverse their direction just in the nick of time and allow me entrance. Some days the reprieve never comes, and I find myself crestfallen as the invisible occupants inside travel without me (surely, I think, laughing at my expense). And when I *am* invited in, there is jubilation akin to Christmas morning and a brief sense of coming home. The story of Jesus' arrival comes with similar rejection, with hospitality that proves elusive, with a less-than-enthusiastic greeting. *No room in the inn.* That is where it all begins. It's a beautiful irony: the one who would set the biggest table for the world and be the most welcoming to the weary finds no initial hospitality.

It's always difficult to be told you are unwanted or unwelcome, to find yourself outside of the space where you seek belonging or inclusion. As catalytic as community is, so is isolation. Either can be transformative. The calendar this time of year can tend to magnify feelings of estrangement or separation for many of us. The closed doors and dead ends and severed ties of our lives fill the foreground of our hearts.

Dwell on the ways you feel like an outsider today, and allow yourself to feel the weight of the rejection and loneliness that you might otherwise avoid. Find affinity in the child who arrives low and becomes refuge for humanity and, in whatever way you can, look for ways to give welcome to a world of weary travelers around you who are desperately hoping someone will make room for them.

Waiting Rooms

Be patient, then, brothers and sisters, until the Lord's coming. See how the farmer waits for the land to yield its valuable crop, patiently waiting for the autumn and spring rains.

—JAMES 5:7

It's been said that waiting is the hardest part, but sometimes and to some people, it's actually the best part. I was talking to my son about the approaching Christmas season, and he said, "I really like the waiting. It's fun." He described the time leading up to the holidays as his favorite part: the anticipation and the excitement, the electricity of looking forward to something and of counting down the days. For him, it's far more enjoyable than the relative letdown of the day itself.

There are certainly times when the time in-between is far more challenging to embrace: waiting on medical test results or word about a much-needed job; waiting for a relationship to improve or for depression to lift. In *those* anticipatory spaces it's far tougher to enjoy waiting and much easier to feel anxious. I always like to think about the fact that several hundred years went by between the Old and New Testaments. What is simply the turn of a page to us represents several generations of painful waiting, of awkward silence, of unresolved questions—which is why the birth story of Jesus is the perfect one to bridge those two parts of the story. It is a wonderful end to a time of anxious waiting.

If we cultivate a bit of faith, that in-between time, even in difficult days, can be a hopeful space for us, a place where we can welcome transformation even with all the present unknowns. Rather than wanting the time to pass quickly, we can actually enjoy it because we know we are being renovated.

This season may find you in painful waiting—in that sometimes frustrating *before*. One of the truths you can rest in is that, as with the child in Mary's womb and the groaning world enduring those long months, there is alway change taking place, always new life about to spring forth. As frightening as it can be, do your best to find joy in the waiting today.

Underdog Revolution

But God chose the foolish things of the world to shame the wise; God chose the weak things of the world to shame the strong. God chose the lowly things of this world and the despised things—and the things that are not—to nullify the things that are, so that no one may boast before him.
—1 Corinthians 1:27–29

Unqualified. Ill-equipped. Unsuccessful. Failure. Fraud. Disappointment. Many of those words play on repeat in our heads. Maybe they were spoken into us at a young age by someone we admired and trusted, or perhaps they were labels we attached to ourselves as we made mistakes and experienced rejection. Since we're living our lives from the inside, we're all keenly aware of our own flaws and weaknesses, and that tends to be the way we define ourselves: by what we aren't capable of or haven't managed to achieve. We usually aren't only our greatest critics but also our loudest accusers.

One of the recurring themes in the birth, life, and ministry of Jesus is that the underdogs will save the world. Over and over, the story is that of the unexpected heroes showing up: an anonymous child from Galilee, a dozen teenage misfits, a grassroots movement of tax collectors and prostitutes, a good Samaritan, a faithful Roman soldier, a small faith community whose leader was murdered as a criminal. The revolution comes from the low places and the dark horses.

We can enter this season well by turning off the voice in our heads that tells us what we're not, the voice that convicts us as undeserving of love or incapable of goodness. Yes, you're prone to mistakes and vulnerable to weakness and apt to fail. You're also perfectly prepared and positioned to be a brilliant light in a dark place.

It Is Not Well with My Soul

My God, my God, why have you forsaken me?
  Why are you so far from saving me,
  so far from my cries of anguish?
My God, I cry out by day, but you do not answer,
  by night, but I find no rest.

—PSALM 22:1–2

I often hear people rightly warning against the dangers of the Prosperity Gospel—the idea that God is a massive supernatural vending machine, just waiting to spit out cars, vacations, and other varieties of "favor" in exchange for some seed money and a bit of faith. This is an attractive proposition, which is why it's easy to slip into that kind of cause-and-effect religion, one we hope will yield us measurable rewards of health, financial success, rock hard abs, and perfect children. A quick glance at the story of Jesus' birth, life, and ministry, though, and we should realize we have to jettison such ideas. Hardship is everywhere.

But there is a false Good News that is equally as draining to our hearts as the Prosperity Gospel: *the Positivity Gospel.* This is the version we're most likely to encounter on Sunday mornings, in dramatically lit rooms during stirring choruses, or eloquently proclaimed in rousing pulpit exhortations. It is the dangerous myth that *belief* should always leave us feeling good, that Jesus is the immediate antidote to despair, and that to experience something less than complete jubilation is to commit heresy.

We all feel the pressure to live without sadness or doubt, but that doesn't come from God. The scriptures remind us that the journey with Jesus is just as often spent in the shadow places, the rough and darkened stretches where light and hope seem in short supply. We tend to see these moments as defeats, to imagine that they are places we need to emerge from in order to be properly spiritual—when in reality the low places are where we meet our Maker.

Today, one of the most faith-affirming acts you can do is to openly admit to your depression, your grief, your *not okayness*. This isn't a moral defect or a character flaw. It's your authentic confession of faith, which is enough.

The Sound Love Makes

*If I could speak all the languages of earth and of
angels, but didn't love others, I would only be a
noisy gong or a clanging cymbal.*
— 1 Corinthians 13:1, NLT

The older I get, the less concerned I am with getting
many religious things right. Maybe it's the wisdom that
comes with age, or just battle fatigue from too many
years logged in the fight, but lots of stuff that used to
matter greatly to me on my spiritual journey has simply
lost its appeal and relinquished its luster. These days I
don't care much for having an ironclad theology or an
airtight apologetic. I know many people who have such
things. Now I simply want my presence on the planet to
result in less pain, less inequality, less poverty, less
suffering, and less damage for those sharing it with me.
I want the sum total of my minutes and my efforts to
yield more compassion, more decency, more laughter,
more justice, and more goodness than before I showed
up. In other words: I just want to do Love right.

What I hear Paul saying in this well-traveled section
of his letter to the Christian community in Corinth is,

"It doesn't matter how much religious stuff we get right in this life. If we haven't really loved people well, we've gotten the rightest thing wrong: we've compromised our testimony, squandered our time, and wasted the trip." To many people outside of the church, Christians are simply clanging cymbals, making a loud and loveless noise.

Advent gives us a gift. It provides us a space to intentionally stop and consider—not if we have the correct doctrinal statements or theological positions or belief systems—but whether or not our lives are producing a sound that resembles Jesus. Are we a welcome sound to the ears of those who encounter us? Today, pause and dwell on the specific melody of Christ's life, and listen closely to what your life is singing.

A Real Friend

*"If you keep my commands, you will remain
in my love, just as I have kept my Father's
commands and remain in his love. I have told
you this so that my joy may be in you and that
your joy may be complete. My command is this:
Love each other as I have loved you."*

—John 15:10–12

God wants you to be happy. It's easy to get that
message from a consumerist, capitalistic, comfort-
based Christianity, the variety of which is never more
prominent than during this season. As much as any time
of the year, we're taught to conflate faith and happiness,
to imagine that believing will yield tangible and
emotional rewards. But our faith tradition isn't built on
anything resembling such promises. A word more akin
to *joy* appears exponentially more often than the word
translated as *happy* in the scriptures—and while more
difficult to grasp, the former is far less transactional,
temporary, or contingent than the latter. Happiness
tends to revolve around our circumstances, around what
is happening to us, and it requires favorable conditions

to remain. The problem is that such conditions are not likely to hang around for very long. Financial struggles, physical illnesses, relational challenges, internal battles, and exterior threats are bound to show up. When they do, happiness, like a fair-weather friend, tends to flee. The joy spoken of and so prevalent in the life and teachings of Jesus is something perennial, an immutable, unstealable internal peace, that, like a friend, simply stays regardless of what's happening. It allows us to feel secure in the shaking, to laugh when everything hits the fan, and to experience abundance even when we should be lacking. Today, don't feel any pressure to be happy, but do feel invited into great joy.

Getting Low

*At that time the disciples came to Jesus and
asked, "Who, then, is the greatest in the kingdom
of heaven?" He called a little child to him, and
placed the child among them. And he said: "Truly
I tell you, unless you change and become like
little children, you will never enter the kingdom
of heaven. Therefore, whoever takes the lowly
position of this child is the greatest in the
kingdom of heaven. And whoever welcomes one
such child in my name welcomes me."*

—Matthew 18:1–5

A woman from our church was having a conversation
with a friend whom she confessed she had been trying
to better understand, as their politics were diametrically
opposite in many areas—most notably race. In a quiet
moment during one spirited exchange about the unrest
following the marches in Charlottesville, the friend
(who is white) said to her with what seemed like genuine
frustration, "I just don't understand why God made
other races." She continued, "If He hadn't, everyone
would get along."

The woman's comment was revelatory. She considers hers the default pigmentation, and anyone of another color is an augmentation. While she honestly laments the division in the world, she doesn't realize that she approaches that division incorrectly, feeling elevated above other people. Each of us has blind spots: the places where we don't see our prejudice or privilege.

As a white, cisgender-heterosexual Christian male, I've never had to take the lowest place. Even when I've made an effort to recognize the advantage I was born into and have lived within, I've done so while still being the beneficiary of a system that declares me the baseline norm—and this is always going to be an obstacle for me. Most of us enjoy some level of elevated status, some preferential treatment because of our nation of origin, our sexuality, our gender, or our very physicality. The kind of humility and smallness that Jesus calls us to is often hindered by the buffers that prevent us from getting as low as he requires.

Today, reflect on the realities of your identity that protect you from adversity. Listen to stories that are different from your own, and find compassion for those who may be more vulnerable than you are.

Beautiful Pain

*And we boast in the hope of the glory of
God. Not only so, but we also glory in our
sufferings, because we know that suffering
produces perseverance; perseverance, character;
and character, hope.*

—ROMANS 5:2–4

The day our first child, Noah, was born, I remember
our getting ready to head to the hospital. We'd been
preparing for this moment for the previous nine
months: faithfully attending our doctor visits and
preparatory classes, making all the renovations to the
house, and packing the bags we'd need to depart. That
morning we were ready—or so we thought. My wife's
contractions were becoming more frequent and intense
as we gathered up our things, and I could see her
movements becoming more labored (no pun intended)
by the minute. She was clearly uncomfortable but she
was managing. Then in a flash, a cannon-like shout
exploded from her mouth and she dropped to her knees
on the kitchen floor. "Are you all right?" I asked, as I
held out my hand to lift her up, still in shock. "Yes, I'm

fine," she said as she caught her breath, but quickly turned toward me and added, "You were laughing... weren't you?" I couldn't lie. I was. Not because she was in pain of course, but because the severity of it was sobering, and my laughter was a coping mechanism in the face of some serious awe. It was as if the gravity of the moment was clear in a way it hadn't been before: this would be a beautiful and difficult day.

As much joy as there is in this season, pain is usually present as well, a bit of grief or a measure of sadness that always tempers our celebrations. We can spend a good deal of time trying to deny or hide from the unpleasantness as if it is somehow an intrusion, but that isn't necessary. Instead, we can be aware that just as it did the moment of Jesus' arrival, pain is birthing something in us—and we can welcome it too.

The Main Idea

He went to Nazareth, where he had been brought up, and on the Sabbath day he went into the synagogue, as was his custom. He stood up to read, and the scroll of the prophet Isaiah was handed to him. Unrolling it, he found the place where it is written:

"The Spirit of the Lord is on me,
*   because he has anointed me*
*   to proclaim good news to the poor.*
He has sent me to proclaim freedom for the prisoners
*   and recovery of sight for the blind,*
to set the oppressed free,
*   to proclaim the year of the Lord's favor."*
                                      —LUKE 4:16–19

At a very early age, we learn how to determine the main idea of a paragraph, that elemental heart of the words we're reading, to find the essential truth conveyed by the author after stripping away the supporting or even superfluous words. It would be easy (and correct) to say that Jesus' main idea was Love—but specifically what does that look like? When the rubber meets the road, how are we to live? Jesus' first recorded public sermon is a bold and unflinching declaration of who he is and what he will be about. Reading the words of a forebear prophet, he tells the people gathered that his arrival is good news for the low of the world: the poor, the imprisoned, the suffering, and the oppressed. He will go on to echo this in Matthew 25, speaking of his solidarity with the overlooked "least of these," and promising that our faith is measured in how we embrace or reject them. In these words, Jesus tells us that justice and his presence will always be tethered together. One will be inextricably tied to the other. There will be celebration for those pushed to the periphery—and because of that, there will be disturbance where privilege had been cozy. As Jesus' life and ministry unfolded, those who had commandeered the table would be resistant when he tried to make room for the previously excluded. This is a good way to think about love: it equalizes the world as it lifts the low.

The invitation we have two thousand years later, as we prepare to remember the coming of the child who would be born into lowly people, is to pause, breathe, and consider the elemental heart of our living here. We get to ask ourselves what the main idea of this journey is, and with the brief moment our feet are on this planet—what we will say?

Doubting and Deconstructing

*Now Thomas (also known as Didymus), one of
the Twelve, was not with the disciples when Jesus
came. So the other disciples told him, "We have
seen the Lord!" But he said to them, "Unless I see
the nail marks in his hands and put my finger
where the nails were, and put my hand into his
side, I will not believe." A week later his disciples
were in the house again, and Thomas was with
them. Though the doors were locked, Jesus came
and stood among them and said, "Peace be with
you!" Then he said to Thomas, "Put your finger
here; see my hands. Reach out your hand and put
it into my side. Stop doubting and believe."*
—John 20:24–27

This season can be difficult when you're losing
your religion. When your beliefs begin to shift or doubt
creeps in or grief comes, those dates on the calendar that
used to bring such joy, the ones that once set the steady
rhythm of your spiritual journey each year suddenly
don't provide the familiar comfort they used to. Instead
of being more deeply connected than ever to God and

to your community of faith, you tend to feel more like an orphan, a former insider pushed to the periphery of the party. Having something that once was such an integral part of you now leave you oddly estranged can bring a terrifying existential free fall.

There's a commonality of experience for the many followers of Jesus who find Christmas a new challenge. Their religious muscle memory tells their hearts they should be in a building somewhere singing songs and praying prayers and feeling feelings, but they no longer have the slightest desire to do any of it. There is the pining for spiritual security—and tremendous guilt when that security is elusive.

The Jesus who got low to place his feet here allows Thomas to have what he needs in his moment of doubt. Thomas gets closer proximity, enough to touch Jesus. One thing that can be so easy to forget when we are struggling with our faith is that God is not struggling with us. God sees the cavernous depths of our hearts, the meandering curves of our road, and has a mercy for us that transcends what we are capable of understanding. Because of this we can be encouraged even when we waver, knowing we are fully loved even still.

I'll Take the Low Road

*"But small is the gate and narrow the road that
leads to life, and only a few find it."*
—Matthew 7:14

The day my wife and I arrived home from the
hospital with our first child, Noah, was one of the most
exhilarating (and honestly, terrifying) moments of our
lives. After the noise and frenzy of the previous few days
and being surrounded at all times by doctors and nurses
and parents and siblings, suddenly there we were in that
house—just the three of us. The silence and stillness,
though welcome, was frightening. I remember thinking
to myself: "Oh man, now we have to actually *do* this.
We actually have to *become* parents!" I suddenly wanted
nine more months to prepare. I wanted to page a nurse
or call my mom or sign up for another class.

So much of the past nine months had been
about learning and shopping and renovating and
childproofing. For almost a year our lives had been
completely consumed with getting ready for what we
thought was an event (our son's birth)—but in reality it
was to be here, beginning this journey.

Newlyweds often experience a similar sensation when arriving home following their ceremony. They've been so fixated on the day of their wedding that they really haven't emotionally prepared themselves for the commencement of their actual marriage. The real stuff of life is rarely found in precise moments or noteworthy days, but in the daily walking out of our gradually unfolding stories.

That's the beauty of the season of Advent. It really doesn't prepare you for a singular day, for one identifiable moment, for a 24-hour event. It helps you to see and listen and move differently as you travel through the next part of your journey, far beyond a specific spot on the calendar. Much like my wife and I sitting there in the quiet of that morning, you get to pause momentarily—and then keep living. As you do, may you embrace all the low places: the places of grief and reverence, of caregiving and prayer, of peace and rest. Keep walking.

Christmas Day: Delivery Room

"Blessed are the peacemakers, for they will be called children of God."

—MATTHEW 5:9

Hospital delivery rooms are places where smiles often come easily. They are, after all, spaces built specifically for welcome, and the expectancy when you're standing there is palpable. There's something about a new life arriving that viscerally pushes back the darkness, like the dawn breaking in and sending light streaking into every shadowed corner of the world, erasing the frightening memories of the night. In delivery rooms hope is almost an involuntary response. Though on many days we may struggle with the news in front of us, a baby is a tangible reminder that something new is always unfolding, even in the midst of repetitive pain and injustice. The Christmas narrative is that of Hope arriving, largely quiet and still decidedly triumphant, in a world irrevocably altered without even being aware of it in the moment. A handful of fortunate spectators bear witness to the birth of a revolution long before most of humanity gets the news. In many ways every life arrives like this, with a few people present and fully awake to the balance in the world shifting. The occasion is one pregnant with possibility.

Today I read that an estimated 250 children are born every minute, about four per second. Four distinct, beautiful lives arriving in the width of a breath. In the time it takes to blink, staggering potential is released—again and again and again. Right now. In this second. As you read these words, birth is taking place. Light is breaking in. Possibility is being born.

You don't need to fully embrace Christian orthodoxy or even be a particularly religious person to embrace the dawn in every second, in the ways the planet is always being made new, and in the reality that we get to participate in it all while we're here. Every day we open our eyes and greet the sun, we are gifted a Christmas miracle. You wake in and walk into this glorious new day—into the delivery room of the present. You have this entirely new, never to be repeated opportunity to bring peace and compassion into a space that so needs it. Hope is being born again with the light arriving. Today is a birth day. This is the greatest of good news.